Tender One

poems by

G. Gazelka

Finishing Line Press
Georgetown, Kentucky

Tender One

Copyright © 2024 by G. Gazelka
ISBN 979-8-88838-600-2 First Edition
All rights reserved under International and Pan-American Copyright Conventions. No part of this book may be reproduced in any manner whatsoever without written permission from the publisher, except in the case of brief quotations embodied in critical articles and reviews.

ACKNOWLEDGMENTS

I am thankful to the Unknown God.

I am thankful to Marilyn Kallet and Jonathan Fink for teaching me the craft and kind words. I am thankful to longtime friend and unofficial editor Whitney Jones Francis of Empowered Writing for her continued feedback. I am thankful to my colleague Kara Olson, a poet herself, for taking the time to read the work and giving high praise. I am thankful to Leah Huete de Maines for thinking my work worthy of being published, Mimi David for the warm welcome, and the rest of the people at Finishing Line Press who have been so gracious to me. I am thankful to the many for their various contributions to my life and work. Just as much, I am thankful for you, dear readers.

Publisher: Leah Huete de Maines
Editor: Christen Kincaid
Cover and Interior Art: Gene Gazelka
Author Photo: Phoebe Fettig of Phoebe Fettig Images
Cover Design: Elizabeth Maines McCleavy

Order online: www.finishinglinepress.com
also available on amazon.com

Author inquiries and mail orders:
Finishing Line Press
PO Box 1626
Georgetown, Kentucky 40324
USA

Contents

Storyteller 1

   Image: Sunrise

Magick Hope and Sacred Moons 3

To Be Alone With You 5

In the Graveyard 6

   Image: Graveyard

Shakti 8

Guidance 10

Meditations 11

   Image: Tree

Stigmata 13

Ecclesiastes 14

Untitled poem 15

Bathsheba 16

A Psalm 17

   Image: Mountainside

Pronounced Love at the Scene 19

Vows 20

Unmapped 21

Untitled poem 22

Untitled poem 23

*For those who wander, lost or not—
For my siblings—*

Storyteller

When we were young
my wings carried you beyond
our paper mache nest
  where I learned warbling
  lullabies wards away the dark
  creeping from the cracks in the night,
and outside this realm of terror
     your sunflower hands
    turned my face to sunlight
    and your composit head
  took the weight of the past
and all became travelers' songs,
     warriors' creeds,
     and faerie bliss.

In time,
    in moonlit fancy
  we saw again the willow's tears
     and machete headlines
     drifting in the breeze.
     War looted our home.
Yet in that whirlwind I hope
you still hear my small voice
and come to rest by my fire
 in your dark night.

Magick Hope and Sacred Moons

I.

Now the Pleiades sisters, once hunted by Orion,
once caretakers of the infant Bacchus,
watch over each step Avalon, descendent of Atlantis,
paces to and fro her dear shore. Nostalgia,
beautifully lit by the rain of light upon her,
carries the summer breeze into fall, even into winter,
heliacal rising. In her humanity, Avalon is bound to sea
and bound to land, yet she breathes the stars into every life
she touches, graced with divine purpose. Water flows in her
blood, and each drip from her fingers is restorative.
Selfless by nature, she is extraordinary. Her home
opens in the earth in the evening where she dreams
of mermaids, sea otters, turtles, giraffes, bunnies,
and other delightful, frolicking, magical creatures.

II.

Now Avalon, the most gracious of souls on earth,
who tracks the alignment of the stars with pure love
and an understanding heart, unabashedly crafts the wildest
of bonfires on the shore with the brightest of Light:
magick hope and sacred moons.

Now Elektra, the one true star of the remaining sisters,
comes alive at the warmth of such a soul and, smiling,
leaves her place in the constellations and washes
ashore to Avalon who greets her with joyful laughter,
and all the words and stars inside of Elektra and all
of Creation resound with this laugh, and if only everyone
in our universe laughed so courageously.

III.

Now Elektra, her passions sparked by merely a laugh,
laughs with the Light and everything beautiful inside her, too,
and embraces Avalon, and they laugh together again
and once more laugh. And walking along the shore,
Avalon adorns Elektra with a starfish necklace,
so she will not miss her old place in the stars as much.
And Elektra blows stardust from her lungs onto Avalon,
so Avalon can feel the magick of the day, too,
even into the evening, and it is like having wings,
and in hushed whispers, they decide to go on an adventure
together, and lifting torches from the fire,
head for a mysterious wood, which in a playful voice,
Avalon jokes about the spirits that used to haunt the trees:
fantastical tales of a king she healed who washed upon her
shore with water, a warrior and his dear maiden who rested
beneath trees, beside still waters, and a love child faerie
who floated like Cupid, dancing between clouds, shooting
everyone full of love for each other and life.
And Elektra "oohs" and "awes" at these stories
retold in a way only Avalon knows.

To Be Alone With You

we all seek places
where who we are
is enough
where we can be
vulnerable
and in being
vulnerable
change ourselves
into something
soft, gentle,
and strong

In the Graveyard

edges of fall leaves singed by the heat of my body
cooled by falling snow imploding around electricity
sharply lancing like neon lights flickering in a thousand
lost souls in the graveyard near the tracks where I awoke
to the metallic screams of your whistling tune—
a banshee shriek at twilight—a gasp, a gasp
as in lightening rendering woolen skies in two—
my body there, naked and scarred there,
my voice echoing over and over distance,
a wailing through the smoke come down from the mountains
to blanket that city who still slumbers in thousands,
even as it sears through me, and I claw through ashes
and dust and the very roots of the earth in search
of that shriek that compelled me from the nowhere
where I laid my headstone to rest in the empty nothingness
beneath it all, and beneath it all, it's my voice I hear
and it's an indiscernible noise, a quiet I can't silence,
a clarity too brazen for a generation fixed in vagaries,
and it is truth more audacious than stain-glass nudes
perpetually shattered by insatiable longing.

Shakti

She sashays in red
cast from the ashen haze
of evenings sacrificed to dawn,
Her presence wafting, mesmerizing
as in smoke, as in
the serpentine curves of her body
slither into mine, as in
oh, my God! Spiritual crisis—
now I know why the Ancients
practice holding their breath—
breathe, breathe:
Where is inner peace?
Her words laughter,
a cloying, "I heard you calling,
not yet? Still not yet?"
Her skin scales across my taste buds.
Unpracticed in breathing, tongue dumbstruck,
swallow years spent in heavy sighs
of not yet, not yet,
swallow loss of loved ones and the possibility of love,
swallow home, alone, what compels my being?
And descend into its pit where darkness
sleeps with fiery passion—

how can you suffocate
  with your body, soul, and mind
    rent by lightning in threes?
      "It is good," She says.
  Light! so much Light—
      see eyes gouged from sockets,
        limbs torn asunder, toes
        broken, fingers snapped
        in a bloodbath of bodies crushed
      —each my own flesh.
      Red snake rises.
Now I know why the Ancients
refer to It as an energy coiled

    around the base of your spine—
    a spiritual awakening
    —it's your inner self
      that is the universe
    and when it rises
      its electricity
        in your
        being
    a unity
      of your spirit
      with your
        body as it
      ascends into
        your mind
breathe . . . breathe . . .
  a cool lightness of being
that is the universe.

What I got
is a "whatever"
vibe and a soft
touch,
which is enough.

Guidance

Silence my bleating heart
    on the altar
Sacrifice—it'll have to do
      I'm no Abram's son
      and wrestle too long
      with Angels
      while you wade
      and play along shorelines
The only way to walk on water
is trust in the calm,
though we all know Its intensity
    as wave upon wave
        upon wave
    shears winter's wool

Meditations

        Consider the lily
     that floats
    with the rhythm
     of grace
    through the passing
      seasons
and the meditation
  of your heart
    will give
    understanding

To the ready writer—
Selah.

Stigmata

The rhythm of grace
   flows through our strengths
      and weaknesses
   sometimes transforming
   weaknesses into strengths
      often simply
      anointing
   the blood that seeps
   from thorns in our hands
      and feet
      touching others
      in our humanity
   and keeping us
in the realm of reality
      of our limitations
      of our need for others

as the blood that runs
   from the Source of life
   weaves each us together
in crowns of humility.

Ecclesiastes

Gaze at stars
    suggest
    all that is
    eternal in the hearts
        of mankind
        who is
        but vapor
    on this green,
        green earth
    born of water to be given
        to destruction
Ask why grow anything
when gone to dust and ashes
        death and madness
           new lives tomorrow, a year
           from now, or
        in wrinkles of time
        exploding in all vapor
Ask why any of life matters
Ask when everything is screaming
        from growing pangs
groaning inarticulate what will come
and why does It matter?
        Because It is the essence
        of humanity that directs
        to the Light in this dark,
        dark world of constant departures.

Tender one—
    It is not our universal plight:
       suffering, loneliness
      that binds us together
It is indiscriminate love
      and care.

Bathsheba

There is
something a
rousing about
unconditional
love, a blush,
a peaceful morning
glow, an understanding
soft as feathers, voiceless
as the wind whispering
across the face of the moon
carrying her naked and vulnerable,
sensual and spiritual, fresh
as dawn, warm as the evening
light, trembling in your hands
gentle as a lamb, a gasp, desire.

A Psalm

    Naked and trembling
she unveils
    another delicate
beauty—an offering
    to absolve my sins
in gentle communion
    with the world
where she has led
    beside still waters
as words escape
    in every breathe
thirsting for the Source
    that replenishes
infinitely in loving

Pronounced Love at the Scene

The morning sunlight
shifts through the blinds
and I swallow my once great fear
of words—that I might never
get the words right—that I might
pronounce "specifically" as "Pacifically"
in front of people and be an embarrassment—
that for all the words I know, the one word
that matters most might get stuck on my tongue
when it matters most, and I type: LOVE

Vows

I will catch the tears
   streaming like rivers
   down your face, carving
their way through the ash
   and soot, for mistakes
   and regret are no
   stranger to me.
In my hands, I honour
the soul who has willingly
borne a hope and a fire
   that has been smothered
   each time left unfulfilled.
   I cherish the love
     of them before me
   that brought you safely
     to me. I mourn
     your sorrow over
what cannot be changed.
   I wish for your better days
     when smiling
     does not feel
as if you are being strong.

Unmapped

And who am I if not
    the hands with which I tend to souls,
        if not the body,
        if not my unmapped veins
    stemming from my wild heart,
        the blood in my temples
        singing holy,
        if not the cortex of my brain,
        if not the purpose set before me
(God only knows)

a wounded mind
is kind;
particularly
unwound in a
splendid way
resembling
stasis

ponder the Way
  of wisdom,
altogether subtle,
  the Spirit
that holds together
  everything
  that is.
a ceaseless radiance
  incomparable
  to light.

While many of these poems no longer appear online, the poems in *Tender One* were originally written on a vintage Smith-Corona typewriter and posted to Instagram in 2015-2016. A few of these poems were given as gifts or staged as art pieces in and around coffee shops (sometimes with permission). They deal with themes of love, spirituality, and awakening.

2015-2016 was an interesting time for **G. Gazelka**. It was their second year in their position at the University of Tennessee in Knoxville after graduating. In grad school, they had received a nomination for a John C. Hodges Excellence in Teaching Award and placed first in a graduate fiction contest. By 2015, with the death of Michael Brown their concerns in and out of the classroom became primarily with racial justice.

In their personal life—which is something that cannot be entirely removed from the collective, they were experiencing a spiritual awakening. After a recent acquaintance led them to see the beauty that would come out of the recent traumas that they and their sister had experienced, they were drawn into solitude to meditate, a new perspective on life and purpose. They studied desert spirituality in Henri J.M. Nouwen's *The Way of The Heart*, the burned book *The Spiritual Guide* by Michael Molinos, the Gospels, Psalms, Ecclesiastes, creation and the story of Abraham in the Sublime Quran translated by Laleh Bahktiar, and the Bhagavad Gita.

G. Gazelka, if anything, is a writer and makes no claims to be an expert on religion. Their poetry is influenced by late modernist poet Elizabeth Bishop and beatnik writers Allen Ginsberg and Jack Kerouac. Their online tradition acknowledges contemporary poets Tyler Knott Gregson, Christopher Poindexter, JETO and the Streetniks, T.J. McGowan, Romlynn Ramos, and Isra Al-Thibeh.

Currently residing in Minneapolis, they can be found typing tags on their typewriter, listening to records, or planning their next backpacking adventure.

www.ingramcontent.com/pod-product-compliance
Lightning Source LLC
Chambersburg PA
CBHW022103080426
42734CB00009B/1469